SONGS FOR SOLO SINGERS

BEYONCÉ

PUBLISHED BY

WISE PUBLICATIONS
14-15 BERNERS STREET, LONDON W1T 3LJ, UK

EXCLUSIVE DISTRIBUTORS:

MUSIC SALES LIMITED
DISTRIBUTION CENTRE, NEWMARKET ROAD,
BURY ST EDMUNDS, SUFFOLK IP33 3YB, UK

MUSIC SALES PTY LIMITED
20 RESOLUTION DRIVE,
CARINGBAH, NSW 2229, AUSTRALIA

ORDER NO. AM999427
ISBN 978-1-84938-383-7
THIS BOOK © COPYRIGHT 2010 WISE PUBLICATIONS,
A DIVISION OF MUSIC SALES LIMITED.

EDITED BY LIZZIE MOORE.
CD RECORDED & PERFORMED BY PAUL HONEY.
CD RECORDED, MIXED & MASTERED BY JONAS PERSSON.
COVER DESIGNED BY LIZZIE BARRAND.

PHOTOGRAPHS:
PG 3 © PICG/LFI
PG 4 © 2009 GETTY IMAGES
PG 26 & 27 © KEVIN MAZUR/WIRE IMAGE

PRINTED IN THE EU

WWW.MUSICSALES.COM

**PLEASE CHECK FOR
CD/CD-ROM
ON RETURN**

YOUR GUARANTEE OF QUALITY
AS PUBLISHERS, WE STRIVE TO PRODUCE EVERY BOOK
TO THE HIGHEST COMMERCIAL STANDARDS.
THE MUSIC HAS BEEN FRESHLY ENGRAVED AND THE BOOK HAS
BEEN CAREFULLY DESIGNED TO MINIMISE AWKWARD PAGE TURNS
AND TO MAKE PLAYING FROM IT A REAL PLEASURE.
PARTICULAR CARE HAS BEEN GIVEN TO SPECIFYING ACID-FREE,
NEUTRAL-SIZED PAPER MADE FROM PULPS WHICH HAVE NOT BEEN
ELEMENTAL CHLORINE BLEACHED. THIS PULP IS FROM FARMED
SUSTAINABLE FORESTS AND WAS PRODUCED WITH SPECIAL REGARD
FOR THE ENVIRONMENT.
THROUGHOUT, THE PRINTING AND BINDING HAVE BEEN PLANNED
TO ENSURE A STURDY, ATTRACTIVE PUBLICATION WHICH SHOULD
GIVE YEARS OF ENJOYMENT.
IF YOUR COPY FAILS TO MEET OUR HIGH STANDARDS,
PLEASE INFORM US AND WE WILL GLADLY REPLACE IT.

IF I WERE A BOY

If I were a boy
Even just for a day
I'd roll outta bed in the morning
And throw on what I wanted, then go
Drink beer with the guys
And chase after girls
I'd kick it with who I wanted
And I'd never get confronted for it
'Cause they'd stick up for me

If I were a boy
I think I could understand
How it feels to love a girl
I swear I'd be a better man
I'd listen to her
'Cause I know how it hurts
When you lose the one you wanted
'Cause he's taken you for granted
And everything you had got destroyed

If I were a boy
I would turn off my phone
Tell everyone it's broken
So they'd think that I was sleepin' alone
I'd put myself first
And make the rules as I go
'Cause I know that she'd be faithful
Waitin' for me to come home, to come home

Chorus

It's a little too late for you to come back
Say it's just a mistake
Think I'd forgive you like that
If you thought I would wait for you
You thought wrong

But you're just a boy
You don't understand
How it feels to love a girl Someday
You wish you were a better man
You don't listen to her
You don't care how it hurts
Until you lose the one you wanted
'Cause you've taken her for granted
And everything you have got destroyed
But you're just a boy

SURVIVOR

Now that you're outta my life, I'm so much better
You thought that I'd be weak without you, but I'm stronger
You thought that I'd be broke without you, but I'm richer
You thought that I'd be sad without you, I laugh harder
Thought I wouldn't grow without you, now I'm wiser
Thought that I'd be helpless without you, but I'm smarter
You thought that I'd be stressed without you, but I'm chillin'
You thought I wouldn't sell without you, sold nine million

I'm a survivor, I'm not gon' give up
I'm not gon' stop, (what) I'm gon' work harder
I'm a survivor, I'm gonna make it
I will survive, (what) keep on survivin'
I'm a survivor, I'm not gon' give up
I'm not gon' stop, (what) I'm gon' work harder
I'm a survivor, I'm gonna make it,
I will survive, (what) keep on survivin'

Thought I couldn't breathe without you, I'm inhalin'
Thought I couldn't see without you, perfect vision
Thought I couldn't last without you, but I'm lastin'
Thought that I would die without you, but I'm livin'
Thought that I would fail without you, but I'm on top
Thought that it would be over by now, but it won't stop
Thought that I would self destruct, but I'm still here
Even in my years to come, I'm still gonna be here

Chorus

Wishing you the best
Praises you are blessed
Bring much success, no stress and lots of happiness, I'm better than that
I'm not gon' blast you on the radio, I'm better than that
I'm not gon' lie to you and your family too, I'm better than that
I'm not gon' hate on you in the magazines, I'm better than that
I'm not gon' compromise my Christianity, I'm better than that
You know I'm not gon' diss you on the internet
'cos my Mama taught me better than that

Chorus

Oh oh oh oh oh oh oh oh oh oh oh oh oh oh oh

After all of the darkness and sadness
Soon comes happiness
If I surround myself with positive things
I'll gain prosperity

Chorus x2

IRREPLACEABLE

To the left, to the left,
To the left, to the left
To the left, to the left,
Everything you own in the box to the left
In the closet that's my stuff
Yes, If I bought it please don't touch
And keep talking that mess, that's fine
Could you walk and talk at the same time
And it's my name that's on that Jag
You remove your bags, let me call you a cab
Standing in the front yard
Tellin' me how I'm such a fool
Talking 'bout how I'll never ever find a man like you
You got me twisted

You must not know 'bout me
You must not know 'bout me
I could have another you in a minute
Matter fact he'll be here in a minute, baby
You must not know 'bout me
You must not know 'bout me
I could have another you by tomorrow
So don't you ever for a second get to thinking
irreplaceable

So go ahead and get gone
Call up that chick and see if she's home
Oops! I bet ya thought that I didn't know
What did you think I was putting you out for
Because you was untrue
Rolling her around in the car that I bought you
Baby, you drop them keys
Hurry up before your taxi leaves
Standing in the front yard
Tellin' me how I'm such a fool
Talking 'bout how I'll never ever find a man like you
You got me twisted

Chorus

So since I'm not your everything
How about I'll be nothing
Nothing at all to you
Baby, I won't shed a tear for you
I won't lose a wink of sleep
'cause the truth of the matter is
Replacing you is so easy
To the left, to the left
To the left, to the left
Mm, to the left to the left
Everything you own in a box to the left
To the left, to the left
Don't you ever for a second get to thinking
You're irreplaceable

Chorus x2

SWEET DREAMS

(Turn the lights on)
Every night I rush to my bed
With hopes that maybe I'll get a chance to see you
When I close my eyes, I'm going out of my head
Lost in a fairytale, can you hold my hands and be my guide
Clouds filled with stars cover your skies
And I hope it rains, you're the perfect lullaby
What kind a dream is this

You could be a sweet dream or a beautiful nightmare
Either way I don't wanna wake up from you
Sweet dream or a beautiful nightmare
Somebody pinch me, your love's too good to be true
My guilty pleasure, I ain't going nowhere
Baby long as you're here I'll be floating on air
You can be a sweet dream or a beautiful nightmare
Either way I don't wanna wake up from you

I mention you when I say my prayers
I wrap you around all of my thoughts
Boy, you're my temporary high
Wish when I wake up you're there
To wrap your arms around me for real
And tell me you'll stay by my side
Clouds filled with stars cover the skies
And I hope it rains, you're the perfect lullaby

Chorus

Tattoo your name across my heart
So it will remain
Not even death could make us part
What kind a dream is this

Chorus
Either way I don't wanna wake up from you

LISTEN

Listen to the song here in my heart
A melody I start but can't complete
Listen, mm, to the sound from deep within
it's only beginning to find release
Oh, the time has come for my dreams to be heard
They will not be pushed aside and turned
Into your own, all 'cause you won't listen

Listen, I am alone at a crossroads,
I'm not at home in my own home
And I've tried and tried to say what's on my mind
You should have known
Oh, now I'm done believing you
You don't know what I'm feeling
I'm more than what you made of me
I followed the voice you gave to me
But now I've gotta find my own

You should have listened,
There was someone here inside
Someone I thought had died so long ago
Oh I'm screaming out and my dreams will be heard
They will not be pushed aside or turned
Into your own all 'cause you won't listen

Chorus

I don't know where I belong
But I'll be moving on
If you don't, if you won't, oh
Listen to the song here in my heart
A melody I start but I will complete
Now I'm done believing you
You don't know what I'm feeling
I'm more than what you've made of me
I followed the voice you think you gave to me
But now I've gotta find my own, my own

HALO

Remember those walls I built
Well, baby they're tumbling down
And they didn't even put up a fight
They didn't even make a sound
I found a way to let you in
But I never really had a doubt
Standing in the light of your halo
I got my angel now
It's like I've been awakened
Every rule I had you breaking
It's the risk that I'm taking
I ain't never gonna shut you out

Everywhere I'm looking now
I'm surrounded by your embrace
Baby, I can see your halo
You know you're my saving grace
You're everything I need and more
It's written all over your face
Baby, I can feel your halo
Pray it won't fade away
I can feel your halo, halo, halo
I can see your halo, halo, halo
I can feel your halo, halo, halo
I can see your halo, halo, halo

Hit me like a ray of sun
Burning through my darkest night
You're the only one that I want
Think I'm addicted to your light
I swore I'd never fall again
But this don't even feel like falling
Gravity can't forget
To pull me back to the ground again
It's like I've been awakened
Every rule I had you breaking
It's the risk that I'm taking
I ain't never gonna shut you out

Chorus

I can feel your halo, halo, halo
I can see your halo, halo, halo
I can feel your halo, halo, halo
I can see your halo, halo, halo

Halo, halo, ooh

Chorus

I can feel your halo, halo, halo
I can see your halo, halo, halo
I can feel your halo, halo, halo
I can see your halo, halo, halo

IF I WERE A BOY

WORDS & MUSIC BY TOBIAS GAD & BRITNEY CARLSON

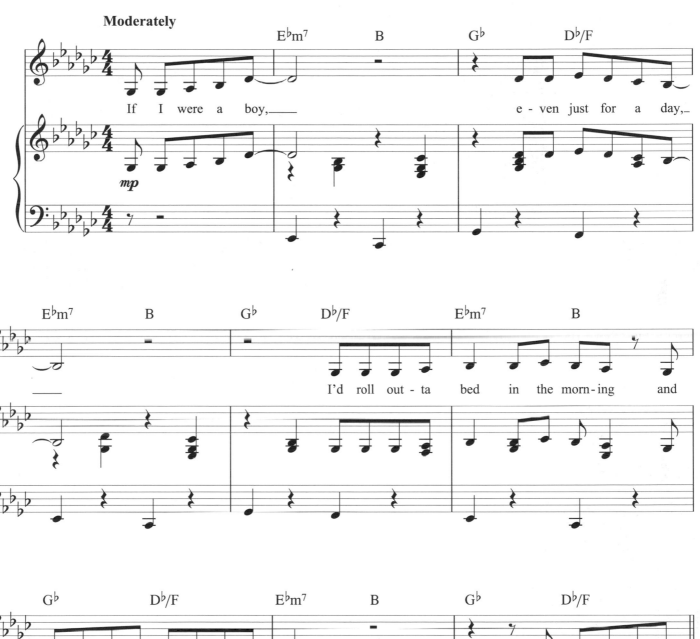

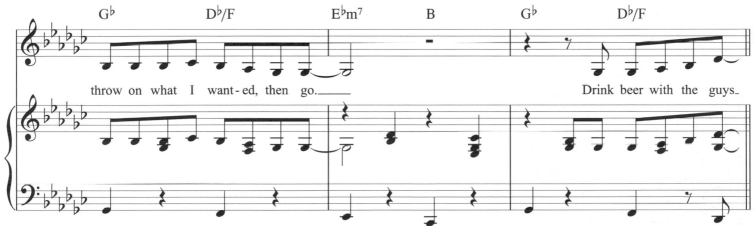

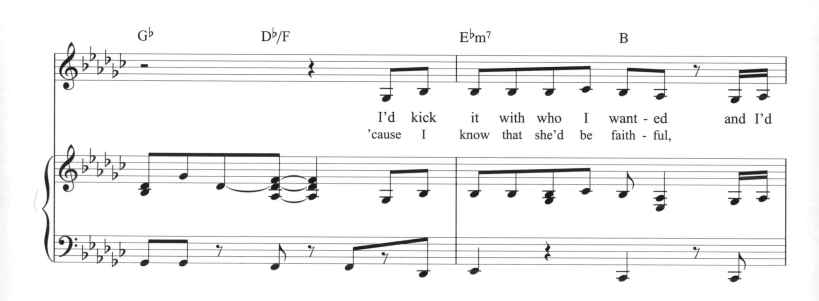

Lyrics:

You don't care how it hurts_____

un - til you lose the one you want - ed 'cause you've

tak - en her for grant - ed and ev - 'ry - thing you have got de - stroyed._____

But you're just a boy._____

11

IRREPLACEABLE

WORDS & MUSIC BY MIKKEL ERIKSEN, BEYONCÉ KNOWLES, ESPEN LIND, AMUND BJORKLUND,
TOR ERIK HERMANSEN & SHAFFER SMITH

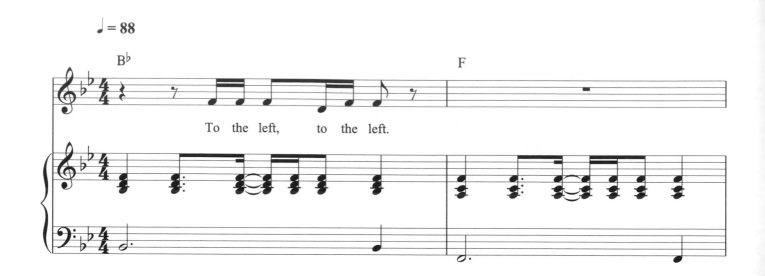

To the left, to the left.

To the left, to the left.

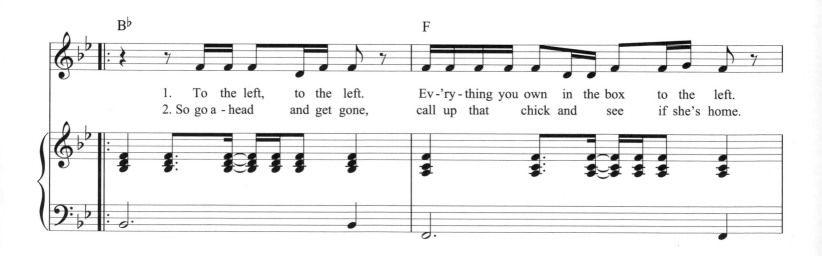

1. To the left, to the left. Ev-'ry-thing you own in the box to the left.
2. So go a-head and get gone, call up that chick and see if she's home.

LISTEN

WORDS & MUSIC BY HENRY KRIEGER, ANNE PREVEN, SCOTT CUTLER & BEYONCÉ KNOWLES

on - ly beg - in - ning to find____ re - lease._____ Oh, the

time has come for my dreams to be heard, they will not be pushed a - side and turned
(2.) scream - ing out and my dreams will be heard, they will not be pushed a - side or turned

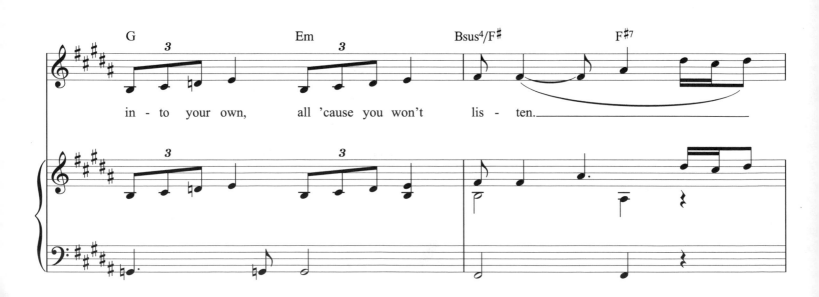

in - to your own, all 'cause you won't lis - ten._____

Lis - ten, I am a - lone at a cross - roads, I'm not at home in my

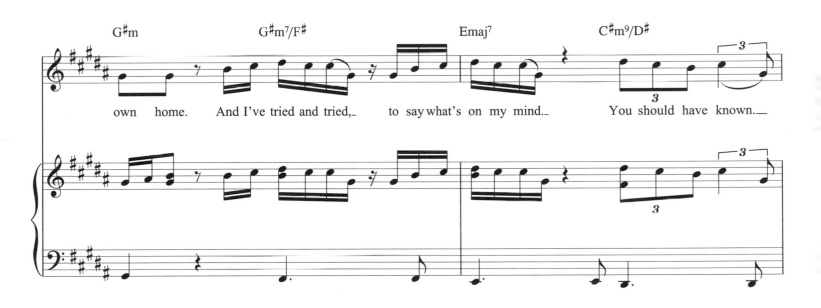

own home. And I've tried and tried, to say what's on my mind. You should have known.

Oh, now I'm done be - liev - ing you, you don't know what I'm feel - ing, I'm

21

won't_____ oh,_____ lis - ten_____ to the

song here in my heart, a mel - o - dy I start, but

I will com - plete._____ Now I'm done be - liev - ing

you,____ you don't know what I'm feel-ing I'm more than what,_ you've made of me,____ I

fol-lowed the voice_ you think you gave to me,____ but now I've got-ta find_____

my own,_____ my own.

SURVIVOR

WORDS & MUSIC BY BEYONCÉ KNOWLES, MATHEW KNOWLES & ANTHONY DENT

Verse 2:
Thought I couldn't breathe without you, I'm inhalin'
Thought I couldn't see without you, perfect vision
Thought I couldn't last without you, but I'm lastin'
Thought that I would die without you, but I'm livin'
Thought that I would fail without you, but I'm on top
Thought that it would be over by now, but it won't stop
Thought that I would self-destruct, but I'm still here
Even in my years to come, I'm still gonna be here.

I'm a survivor *etc.*

SWEET DREAMS

WORDS & MUSIC BY RICHARD BUTLER, WAYNE WILKINS, JAMES SCHEFFER & BEYONCÉ KNOWLES

(Turn the lights on.)

1. Ev-'ry night I rush to my bed___ with hopes that may-be I'll get a chance___ to see you when I close my eyes. I'm go-ing out of my head,___ lost in a fai-ry-tale, can you hold my hands_ and be my

37

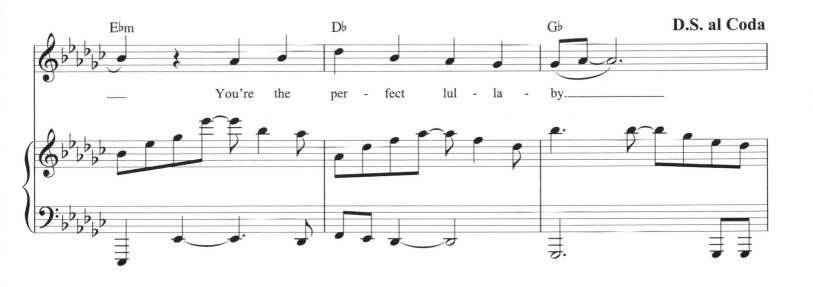

You're the per - fect lul - la - by.____

don't wan - na wake up from you.____ Tat - too your

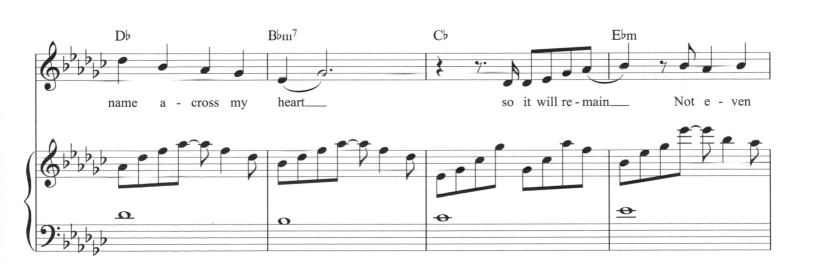

name a - cross my heart____ so it will re - main____ Not e - ven

HALO

WORDS & MUSIC BY RYAN TEDDER, BEYONCÉ KNOWLES & EVAN BOGART

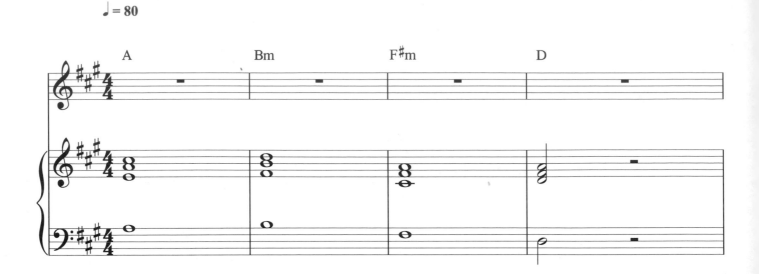

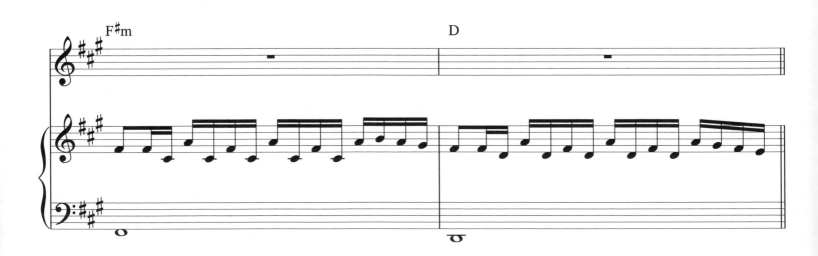